A Cool Balloon

by Alex Yu

illustrated by Alex Wallner

Core Decodable 90

Mc Graw Hill Education

Bothell, WA • Chicago, IL • Columbus, OH • New York, NY

MHEonline.com

Send all inquiries to:
McGraw-Hill Education
8787 Orion Place
Columbus, OH 43240

ISBN: 978-0-02-132388-3
MHID: 0-02-132388-7

Printed in Canada.

9 10 11 12 KOD 24

At first, the balloon just drooped.
But it pumped up fast.
Soon it was filled and ready.

Riders climbed in the basket.

A man set the balloon loose.

The balloon floated higher and higher.

It passed over roofs.

"Cool!" said a rider.

The ride was smooth.
The balloon drifted for miles.
Riders could see for miles, too.

The riders spotted a goose flying below.
They could see a jet zoom high over them.

A first grader looked at the balloon.
It looked like a floating apple.
"Cool," she said.